BACH
CELLO SUITES
for Electric Bass

Music arrangements by Matt Scharfglass

ISBN 978-1-4803-6186-7

HAL•LEONARD® CORPORATION
7777 W. BLUEMOUND RD. P.O. BOX 13819 MILWAUKEE, WI 53213

In Australia Contact:
Hal Leonard Australia Pty. Ltd.
4 Lentara Court
Cheltenham, Victoria, 3192 Australia
Email: ausadmin@halleonard.com.au

Visit Hal Leonard Online at
www.halleonard.com

Cello Suite No. 1 in G Major
BWV 1007
By Johann Sebastian Bach

Drop D tuning:
(low to high) D-A-D-G

Prelude

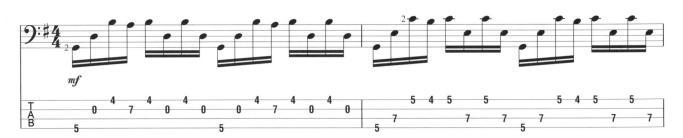

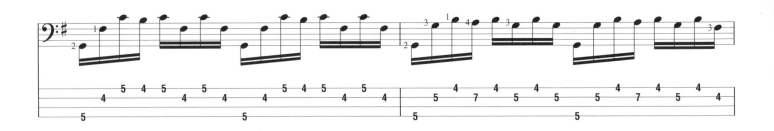

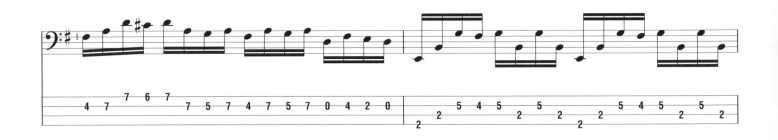

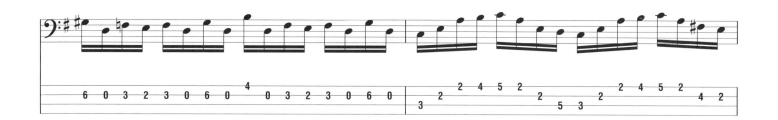

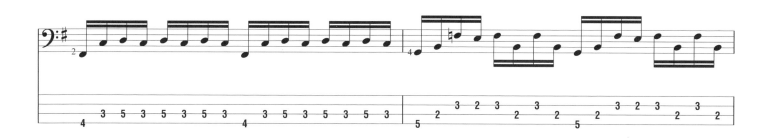

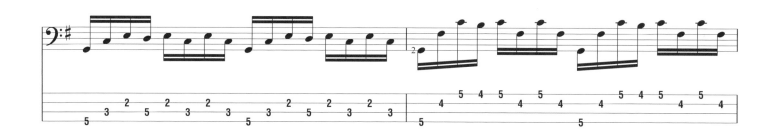

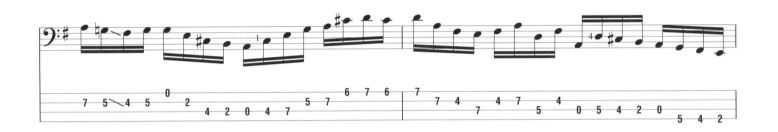

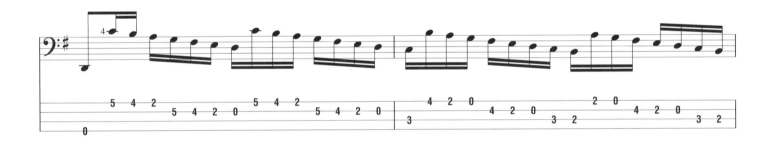

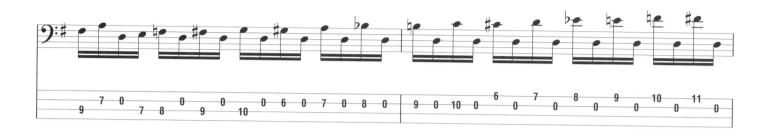

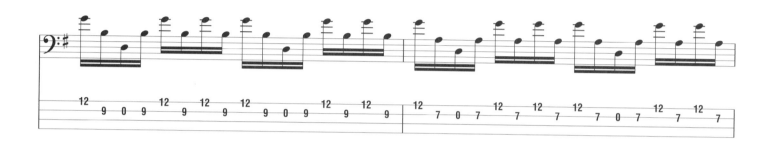

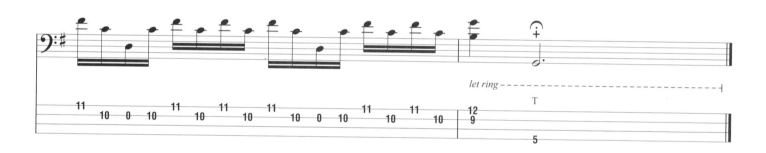

Allemande

*Strum all chords with downstrokes using the
thumb or index finger, unless otherwise indicated.

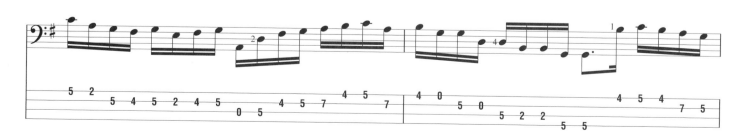

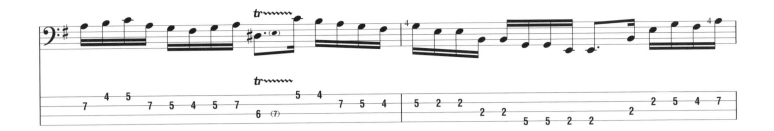

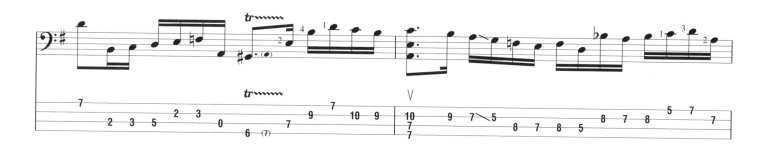

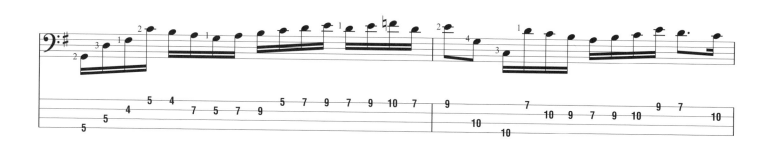

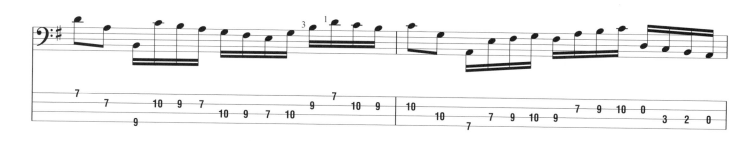

Courante

Sarabande

*Pluck w/ thumb and fingers.

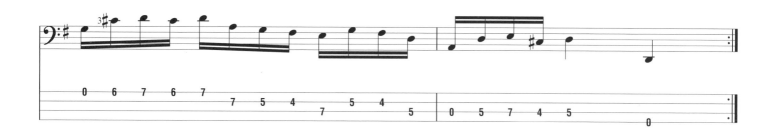

*As before

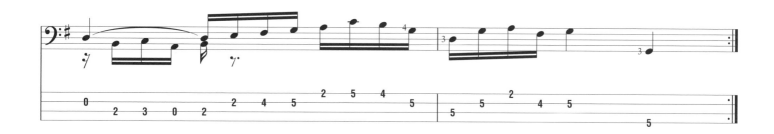

Menuet I

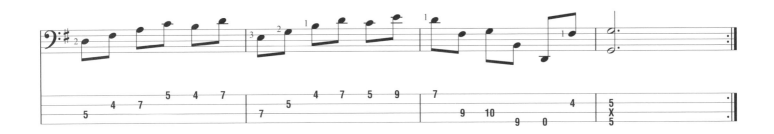

Menuet II

*Key signature denotes G dorian and implies G melodic minor.   **Some sources indicate E natural.

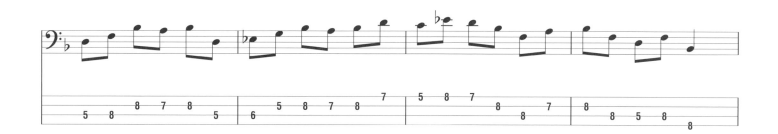

Menuet I D.C.

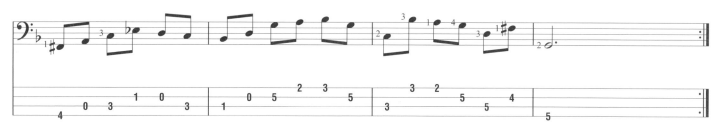

Gigue

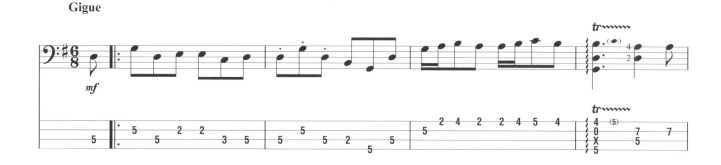

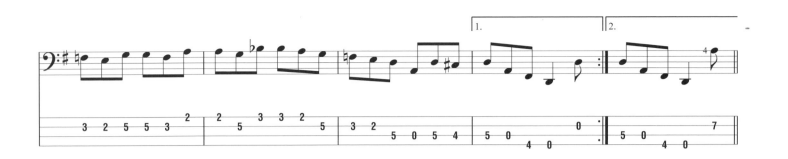

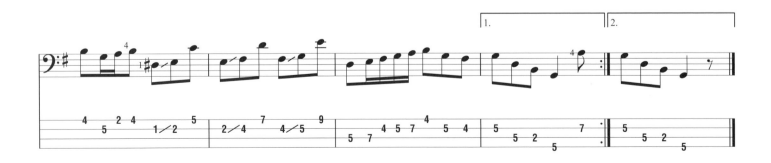

Cello Suite No. 2 in D Minor
BWV 1008

By Johann Sebastian Bach

Drop D tuning:
(low to high) D-A-D-G

Prelude

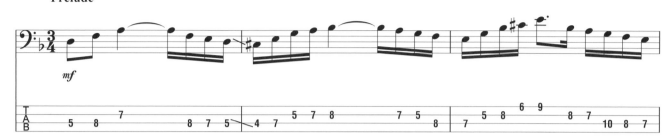

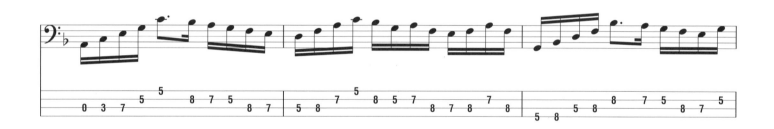

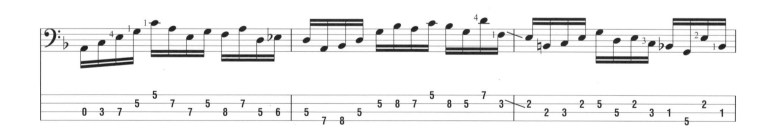

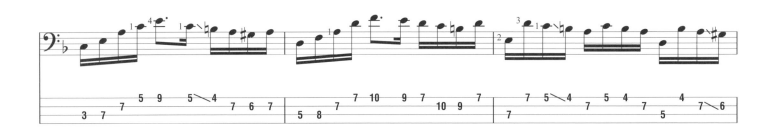

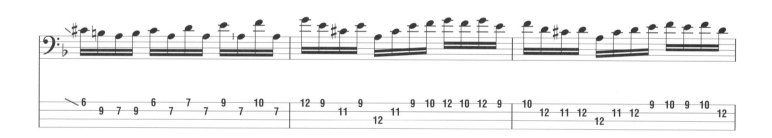

*Strum all chords with downstrokes
using the thumb or index finger,
unless otherwise indicated.

Allemande

*Some sources show F natural.

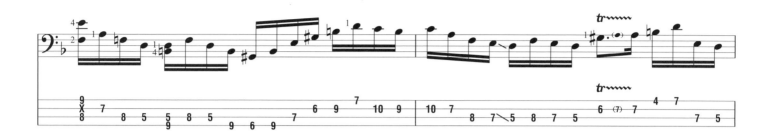

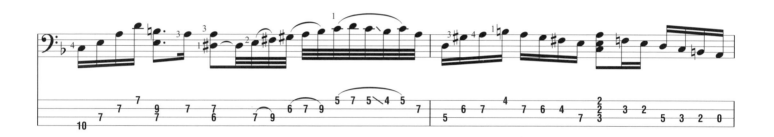

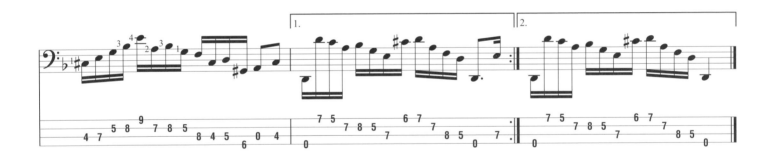

Courante

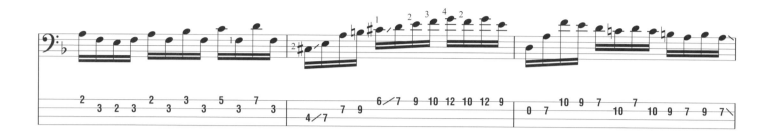

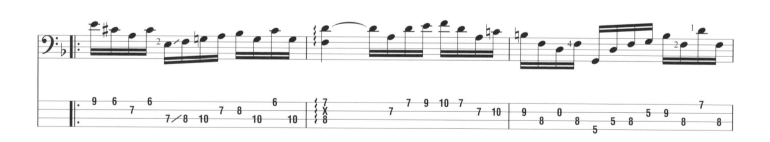

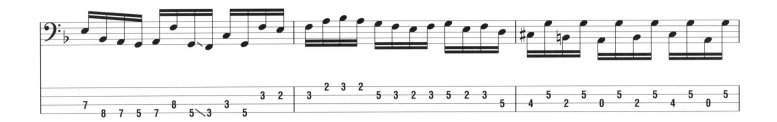

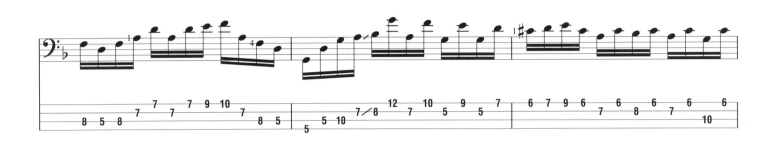

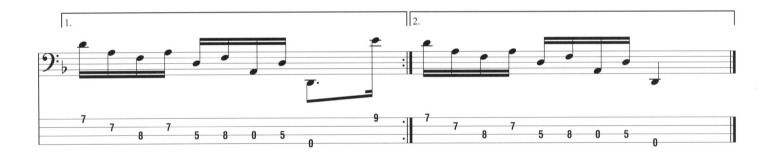

Sarabande

*B-flat is written one octave higher for playability.

Menuet I

Menuet II

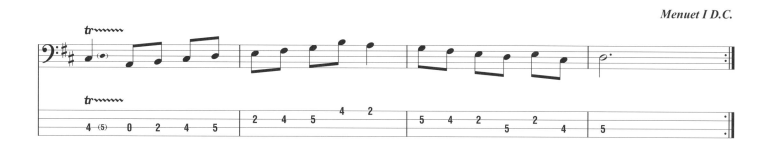

Menuet I D.C.

Gigue

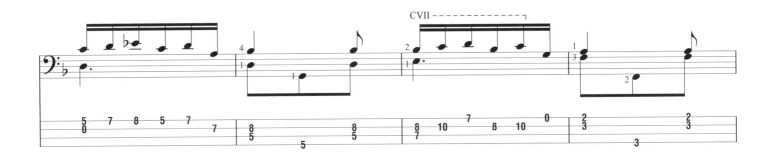

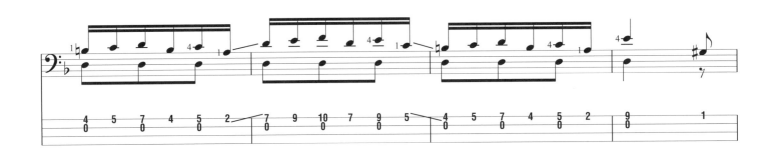

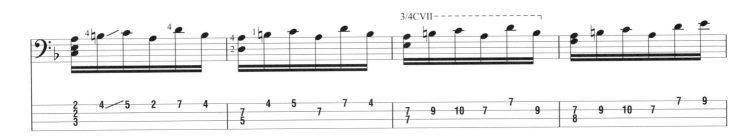

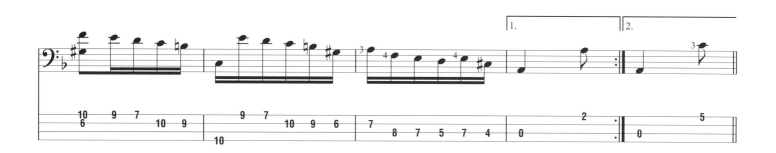

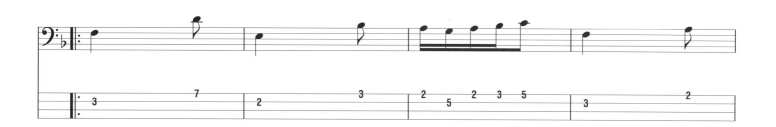

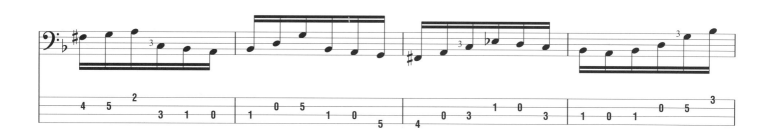

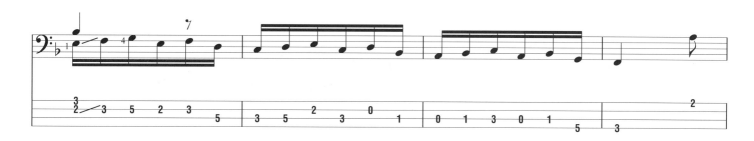

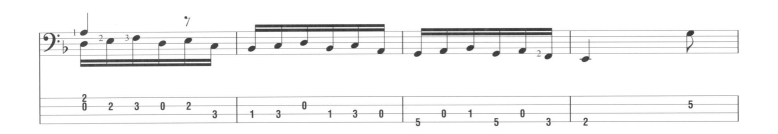

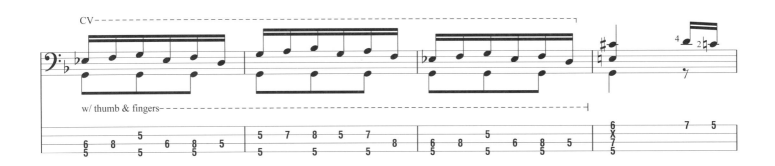

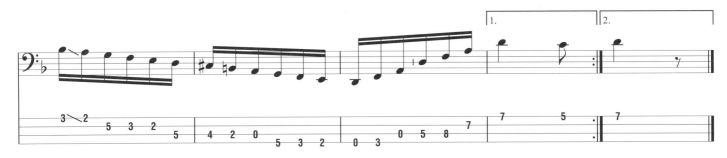

Cello Suite No. 3 in C Major
BWV 1009

By Johann Sebastian Bach

Drop D tuning:
(low to high) D-A-D-G

Prelude

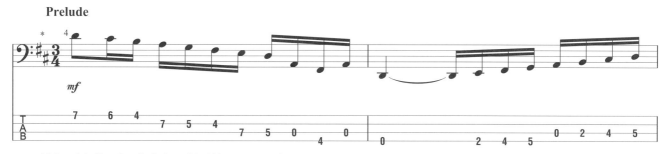

*Suite originally written in the key of C. This arrangement is
transposed up one whole step to D for adaptation to bass guitar.

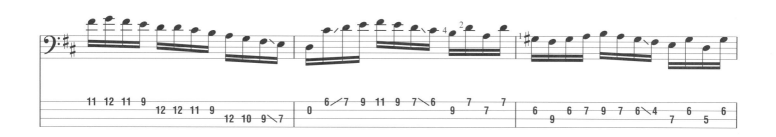

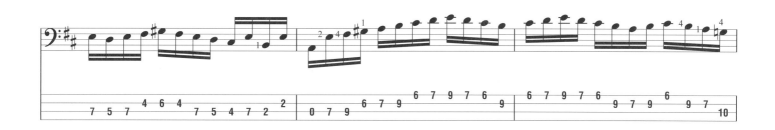

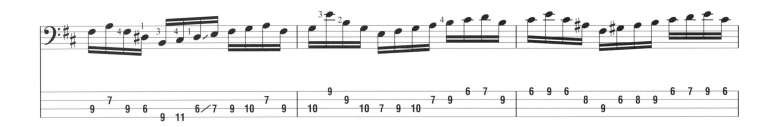

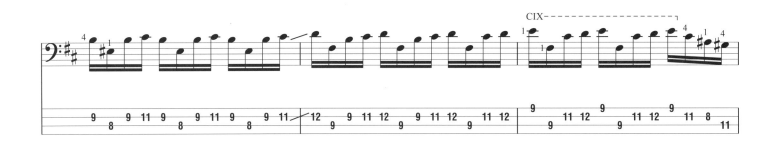

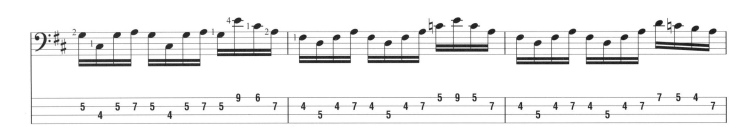

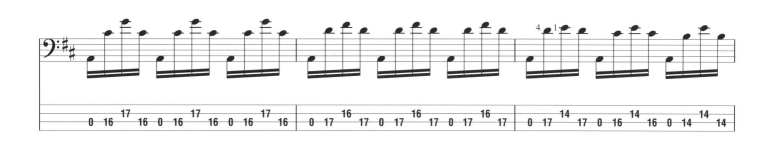

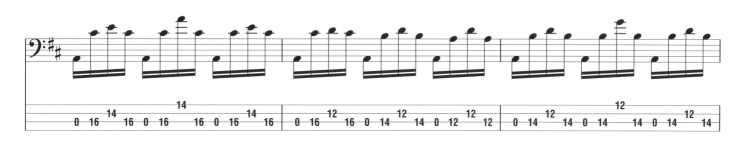

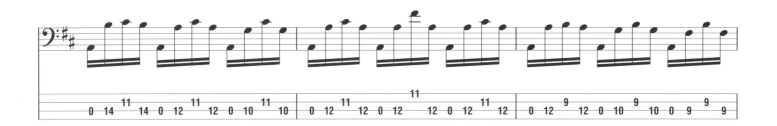

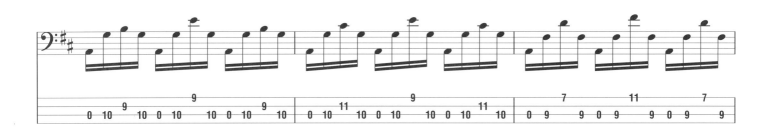

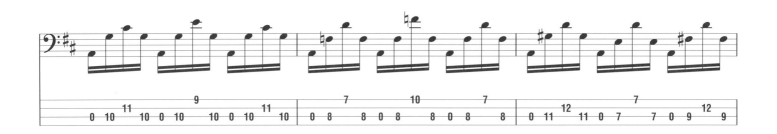

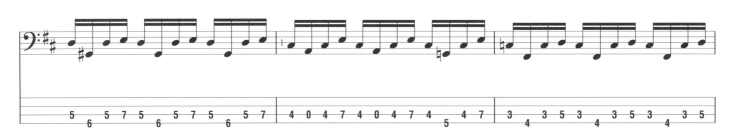

*Strum all chords with downstrokes
using the thumb or index finger,
unless otherwise indicated.

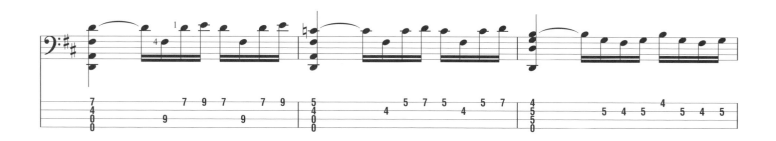

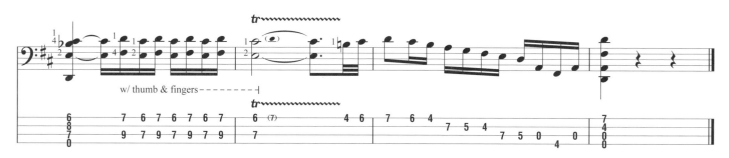

Allemande

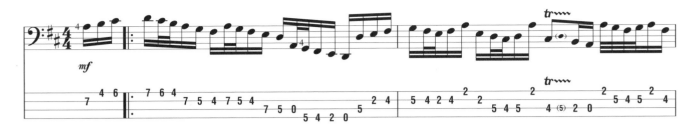

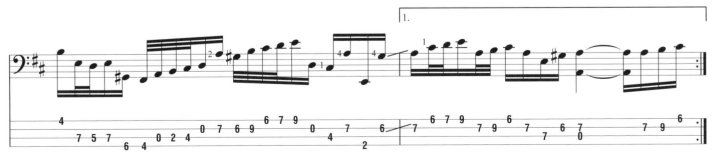

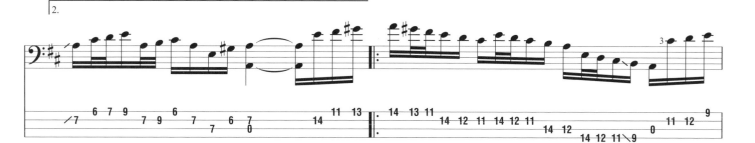

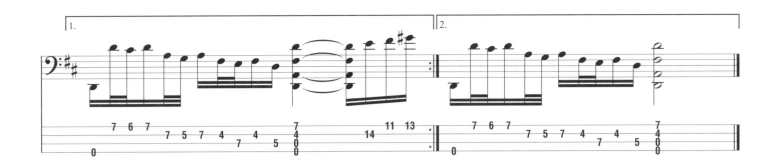

Courante

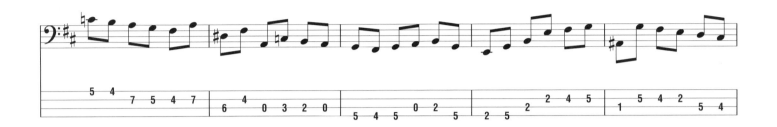

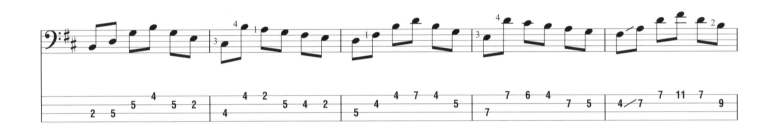

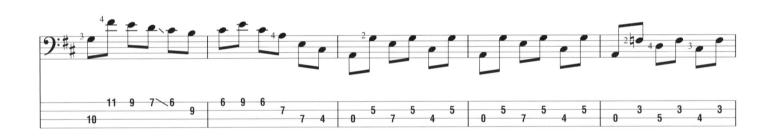

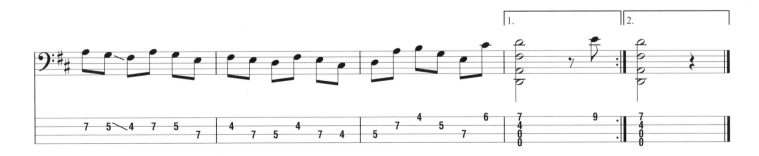

Sarabande

*w/ fingers & thumb

**As before

***As before

Harm.

CIX

Bouree I

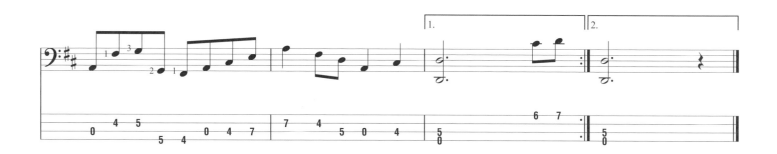

Bouree II

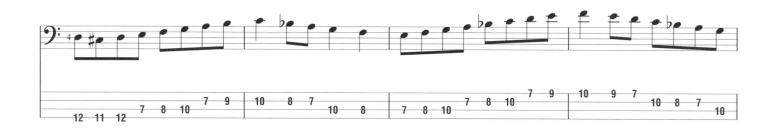

Bouree I D.C.

Gigue

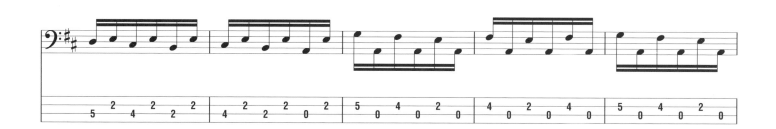

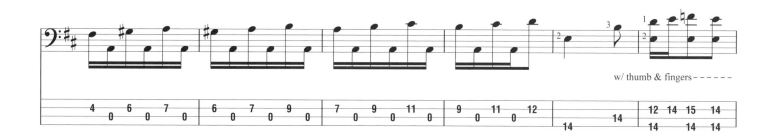

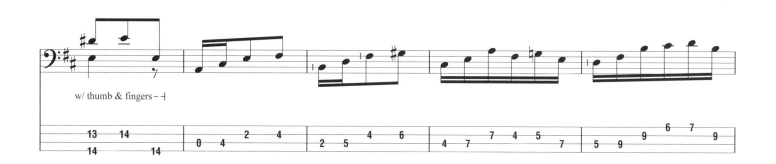

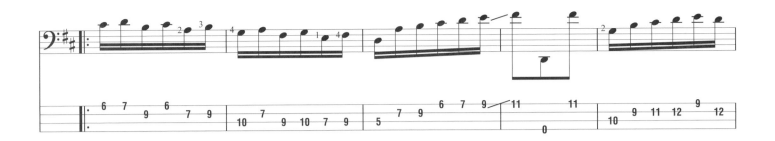

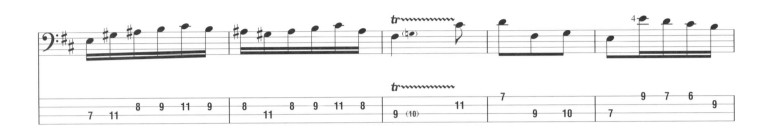

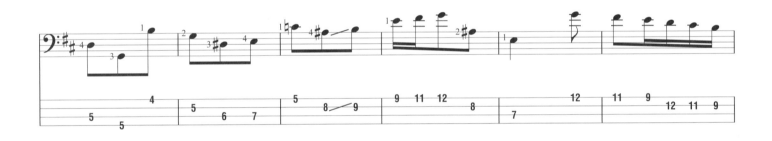

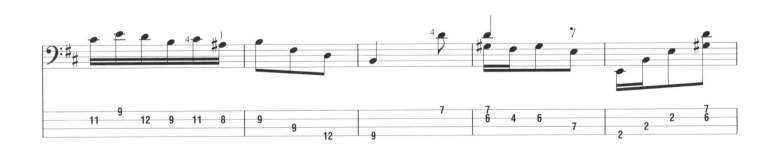

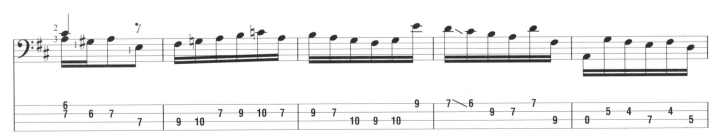

Cello Suite No. 4 in E♭ Major
BWV 1010
By Johann Sebastian Bach

Prelude

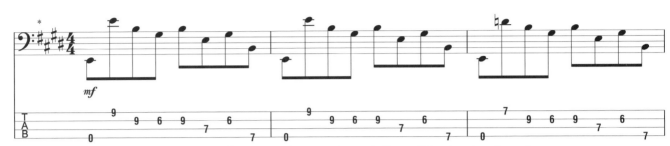

*Suite originally written in the key of E-flat. This arrangement is transposed up one half step to E for adaptation to bass guitar.

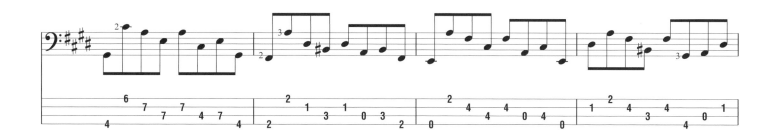

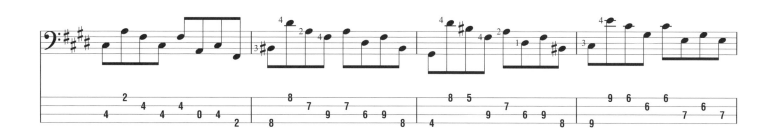

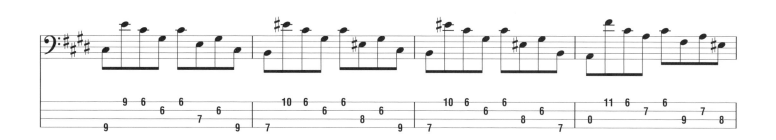

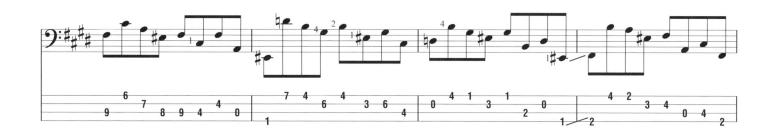

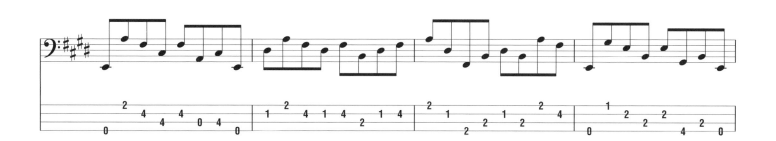

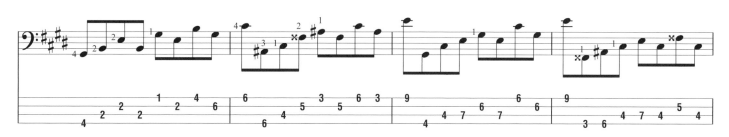

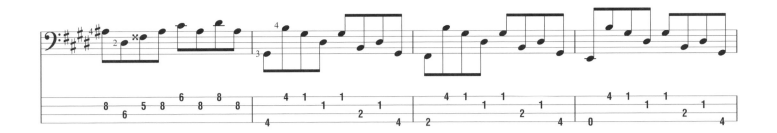

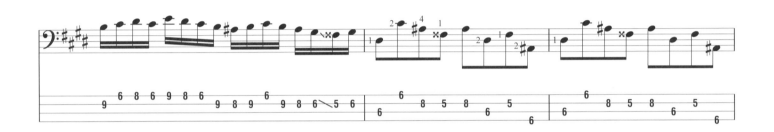

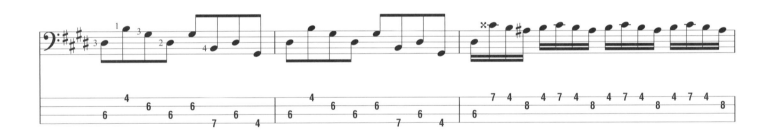

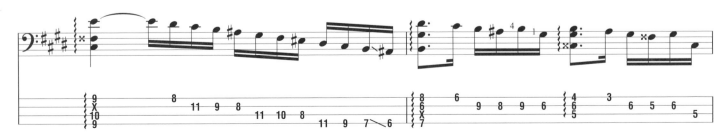

*Strum all chords with downstrokes using the thumb or index finger, unless otherwise indicated.

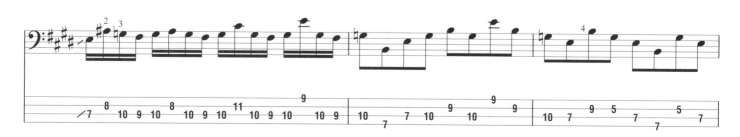

Allemande

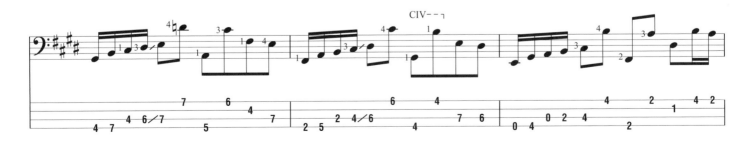

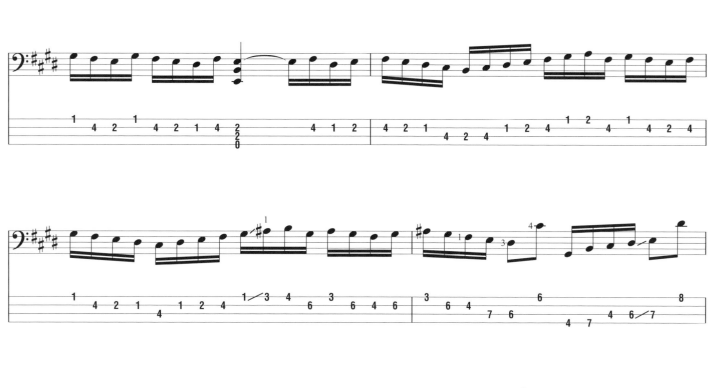

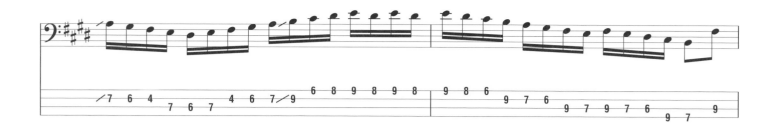

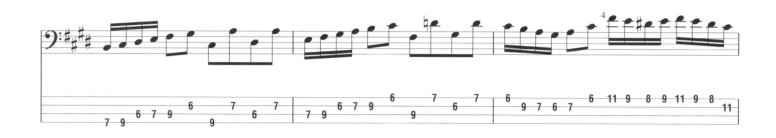

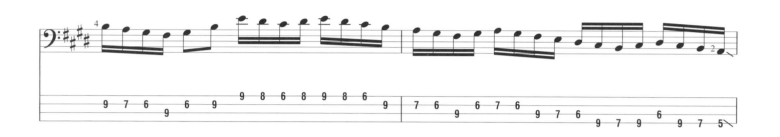

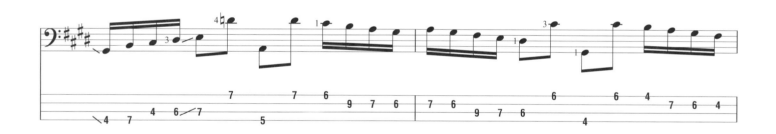

Courante

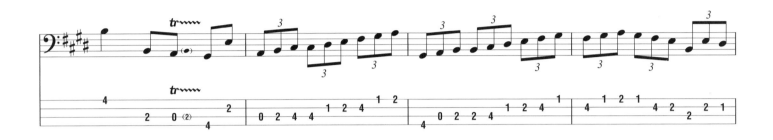

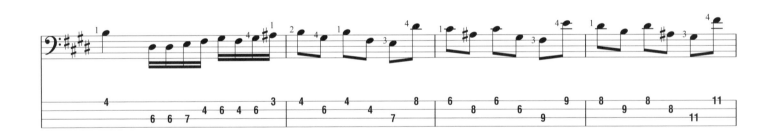

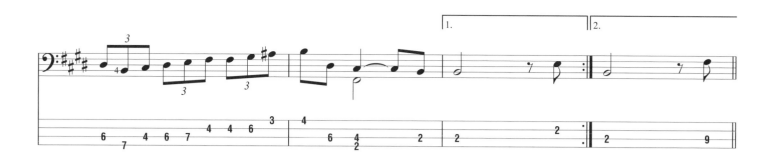

*Some sources indicate a D-natural.

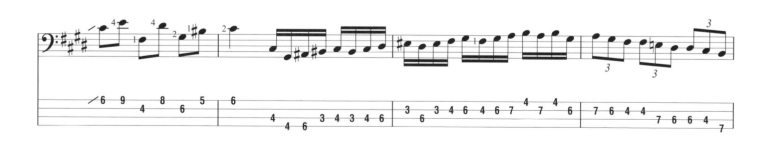

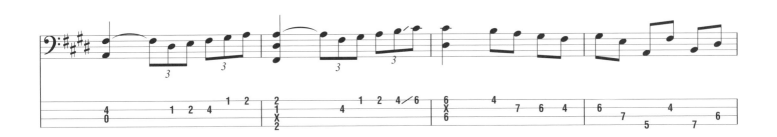

Sarabande

Bouree I

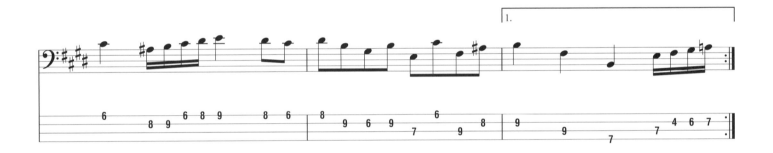

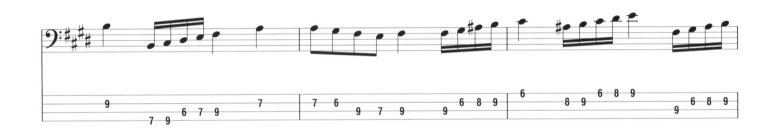

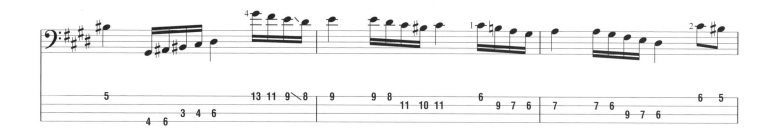

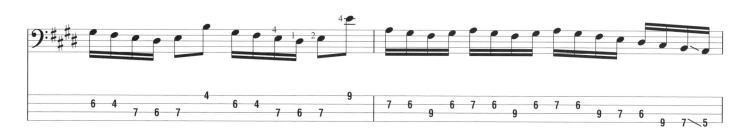

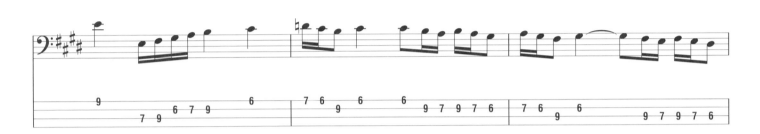

Bouree II

mp
w/ thumb & fingers

60

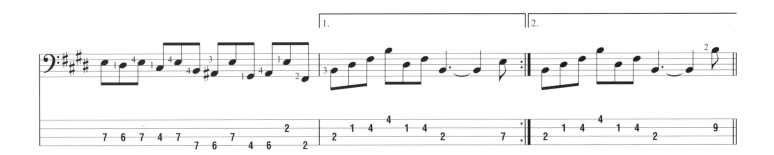

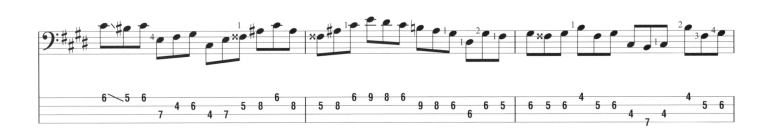

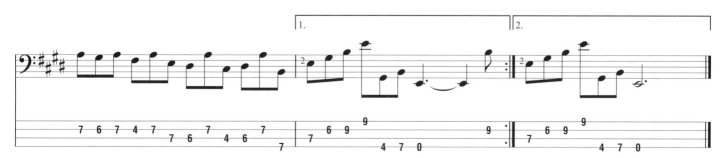

Cello Suite No. 5 in C Minor
BWV 1011
By Johann Sebastian Bach

Drop D tuning:
(low to high) D-A-D-G

Prelude

*Suite originally written in the key of C minor. This arrangement is transposed up one whole step to D minor for adaptation to bass guitar.

**Strum all chords with downstrokes using the thumb
or index finger, unless otherwise indicated.

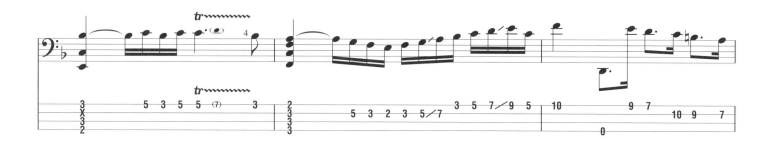

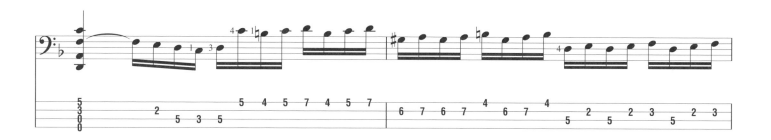

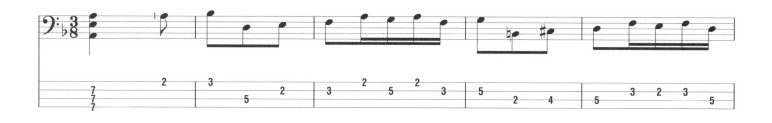

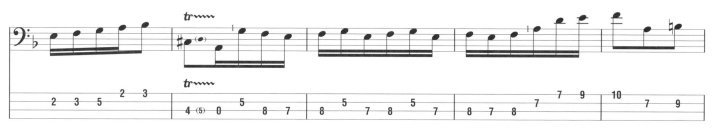

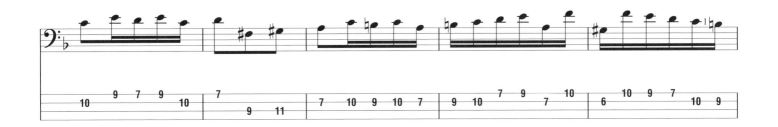

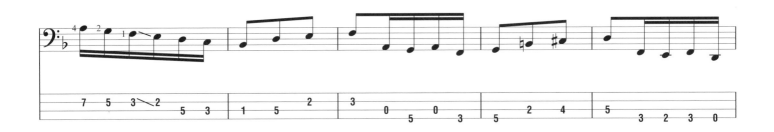

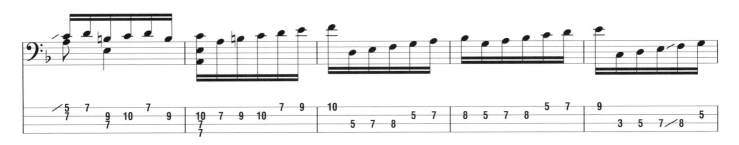

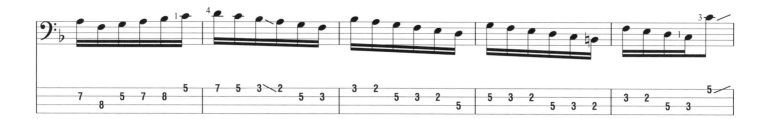

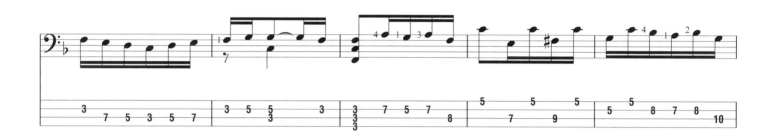

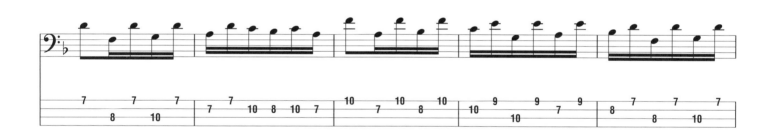

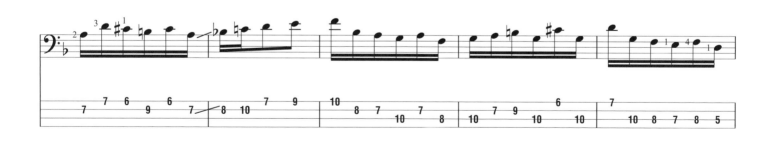

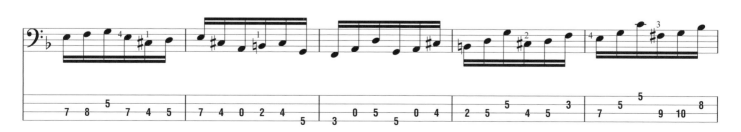

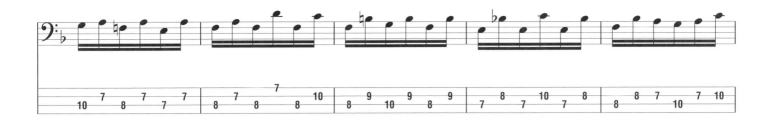

*Some sources indicate a B♭.

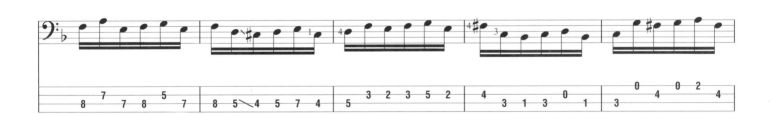

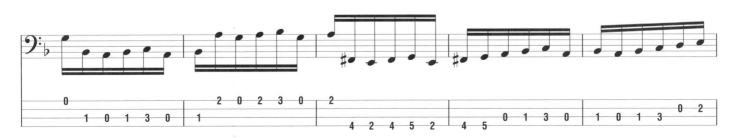

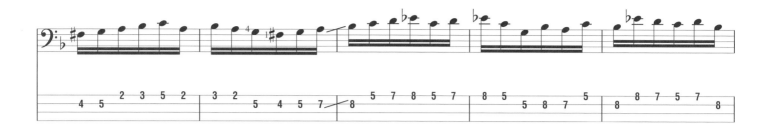

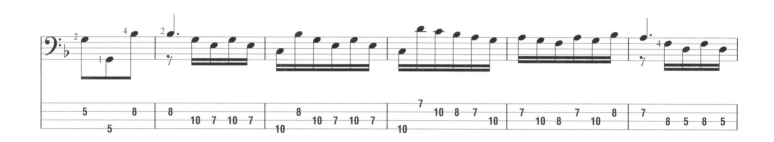

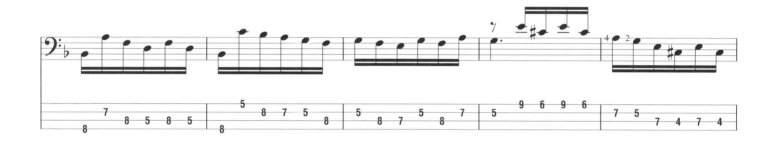

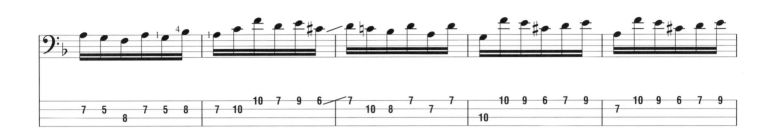

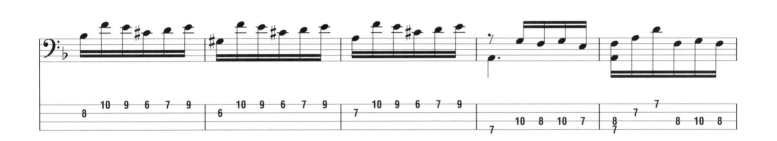

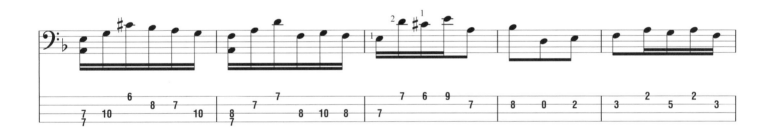

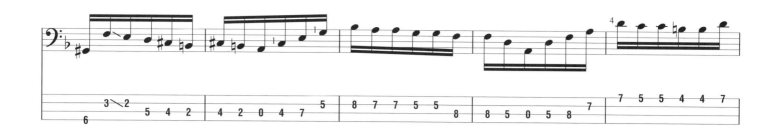

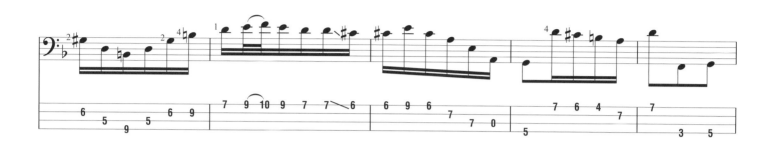

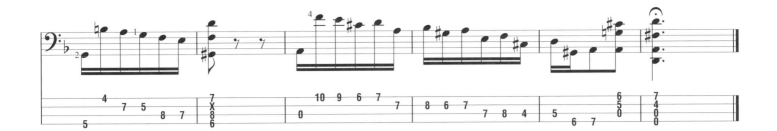

Allemande

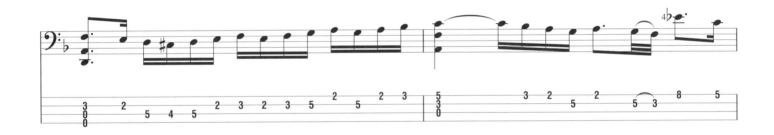

w/ thumb
& fingers–

Courante

w/ thumb & fingers

*w/ thumb & fingers

**As before

Sarabande

Gavotte I

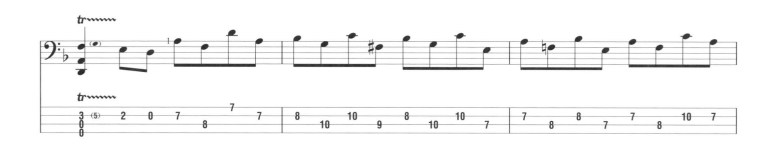

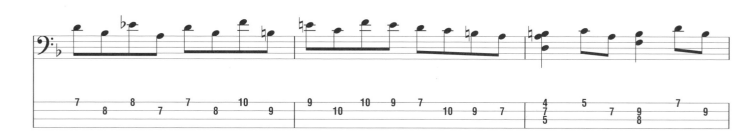

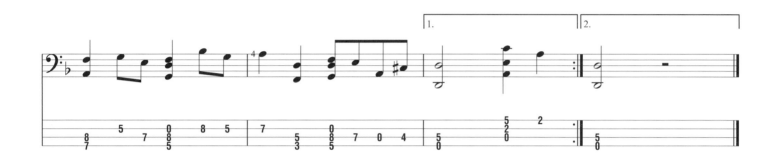

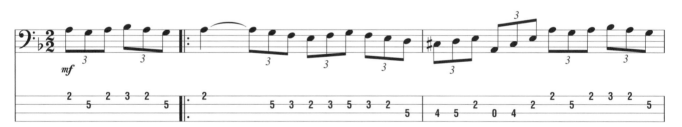

Gavotte II

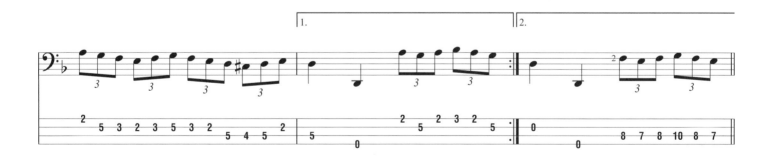

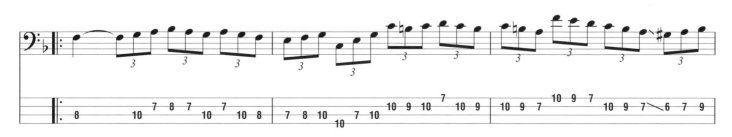

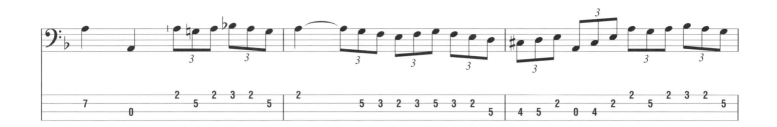

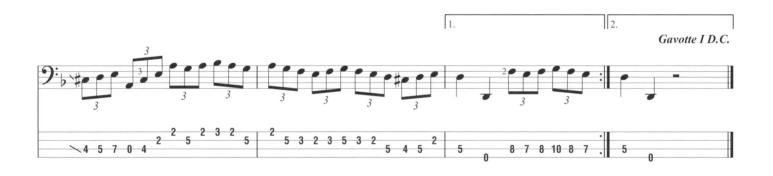

Gavotte I D.C.

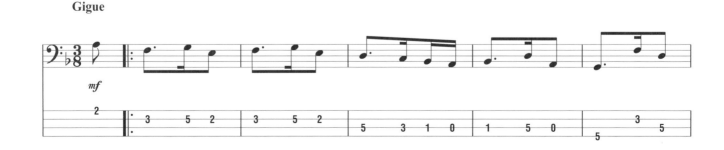

Gigue

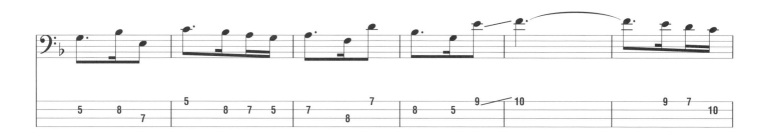

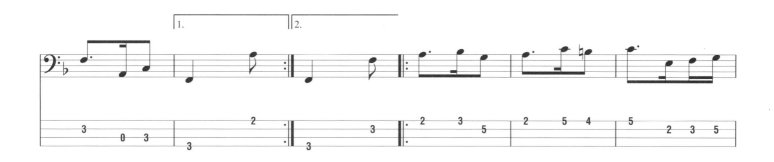

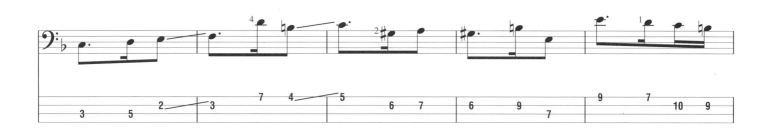

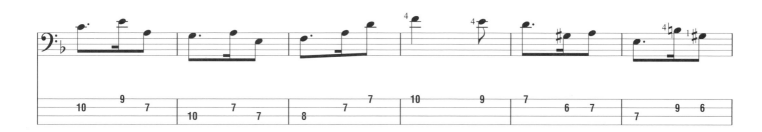

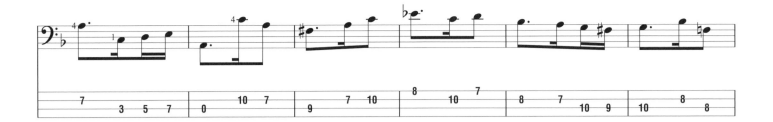

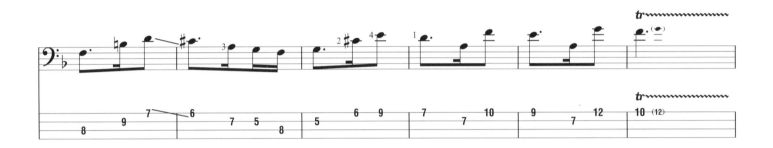

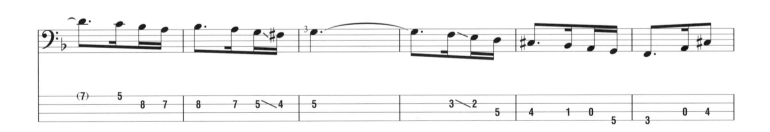

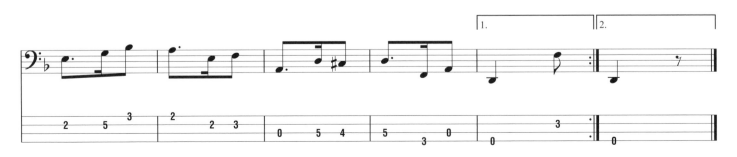

Cello Suite No. 6 in D Major
BWV 1012
By Johann Sebastian Bach

Drop D tuning:
(low to high) D-A-D-G

Prelude

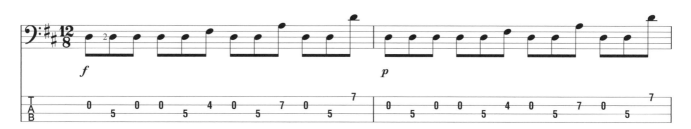

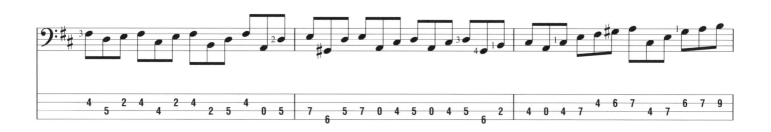

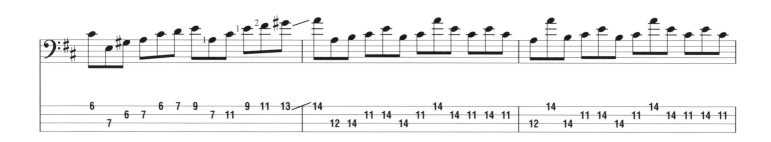

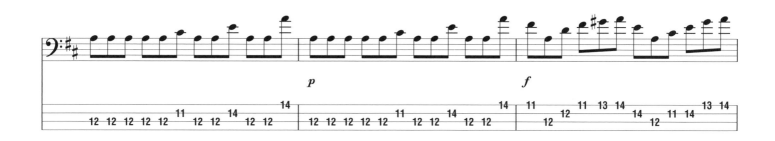

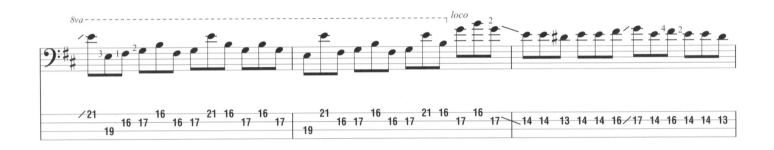

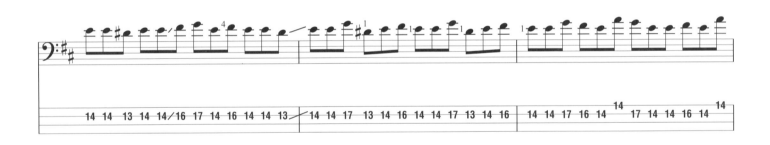

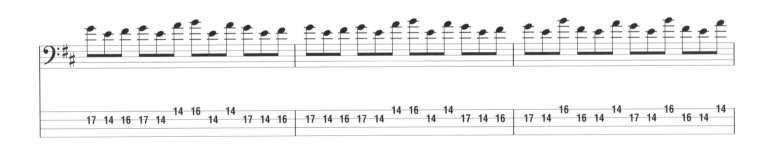

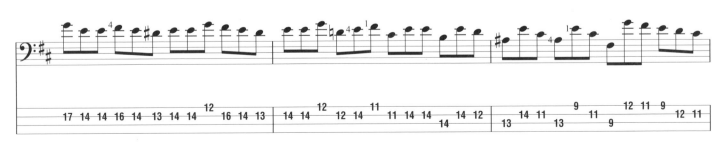

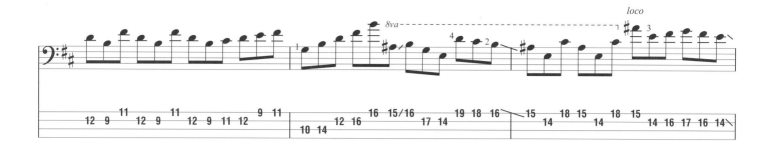

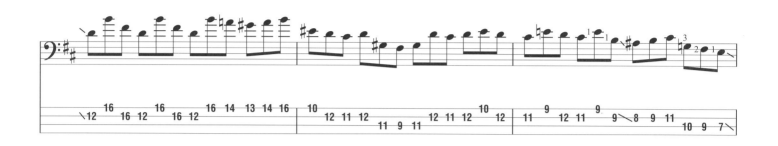

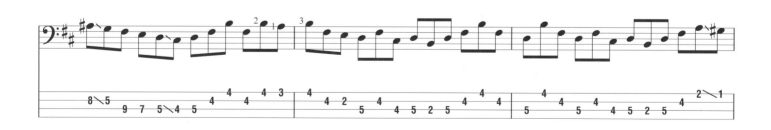

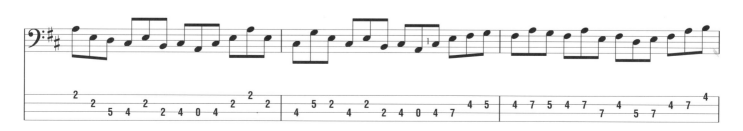

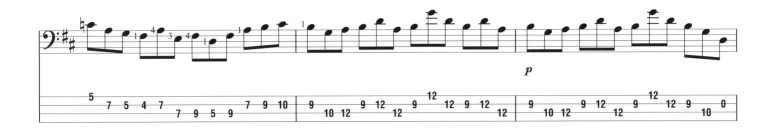

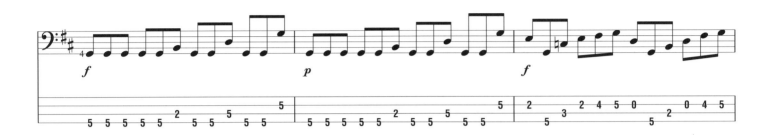

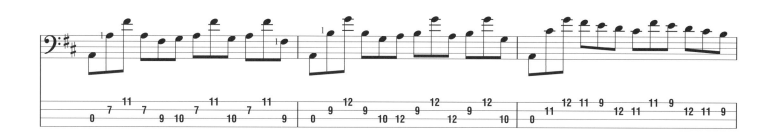

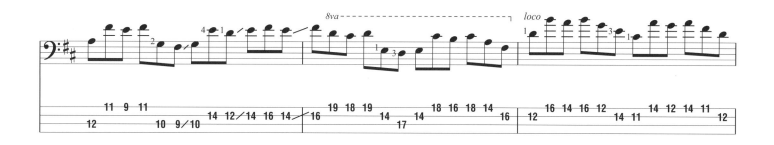

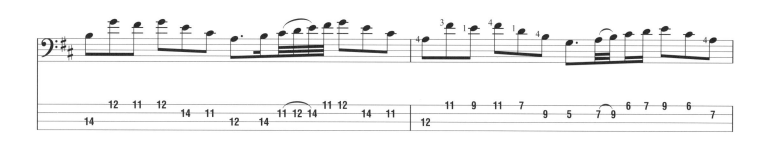

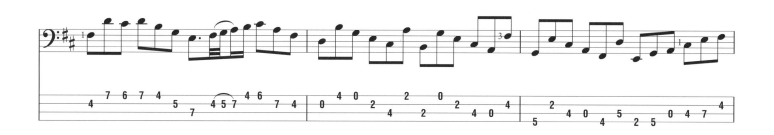

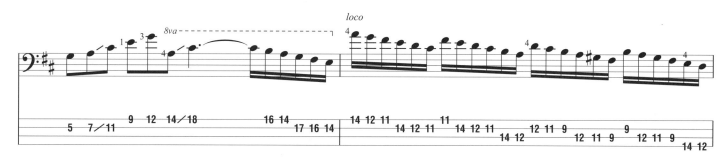

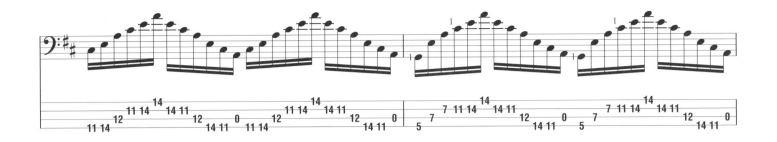

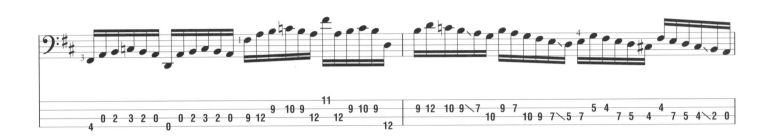

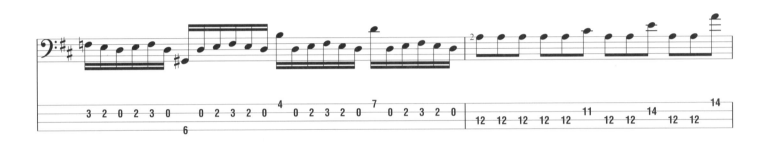

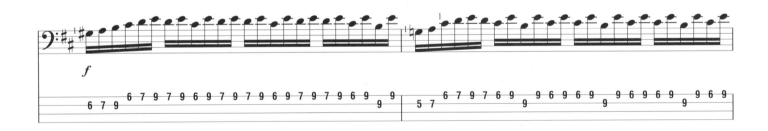

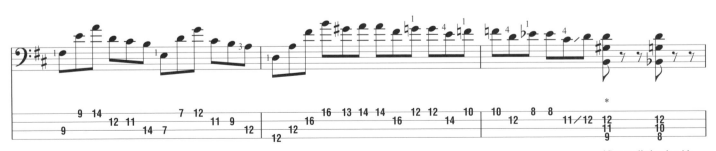

*Strum all chords with
downstrokes using the
thumb or index finger,
unless otherwise indicated.

Allemande

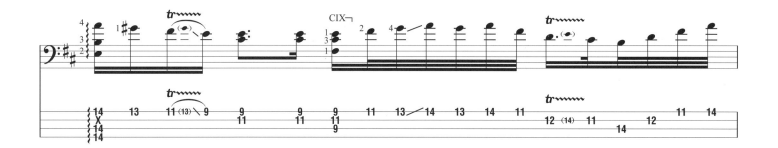

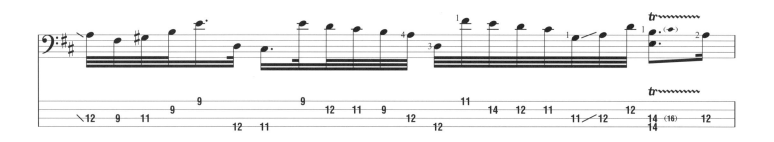

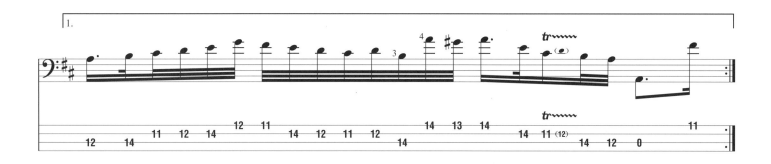

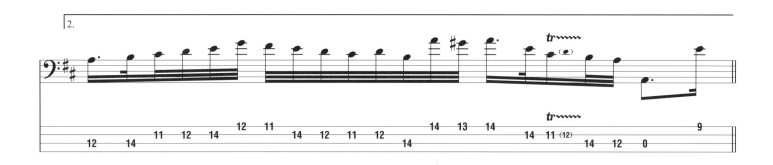

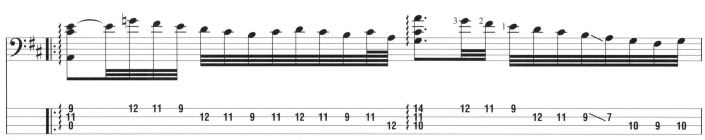

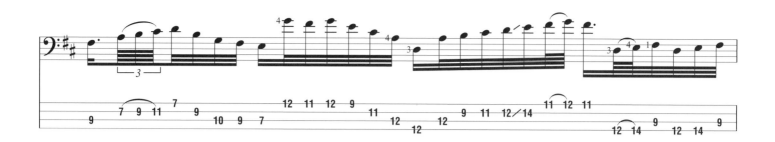

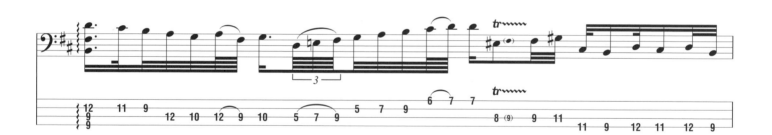

*Some sources indicate
E natural.

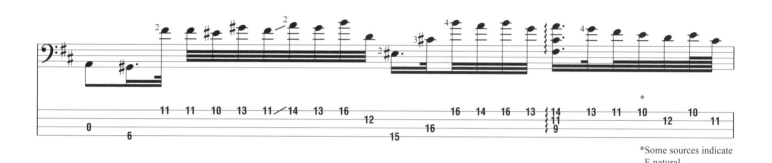

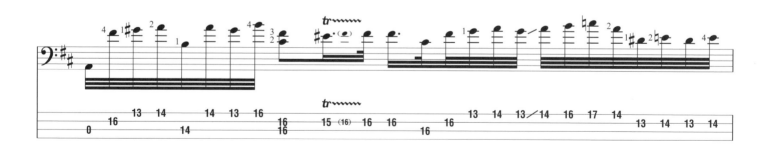

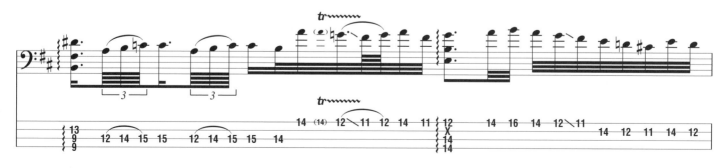

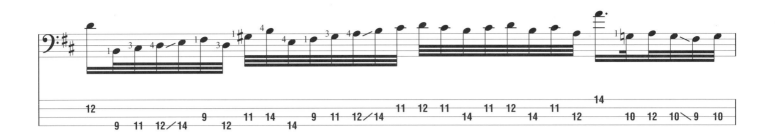

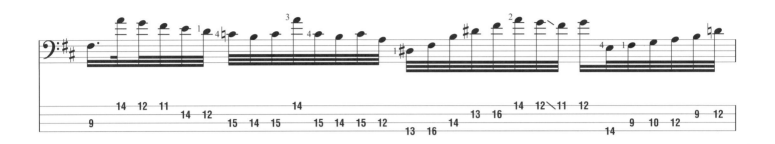

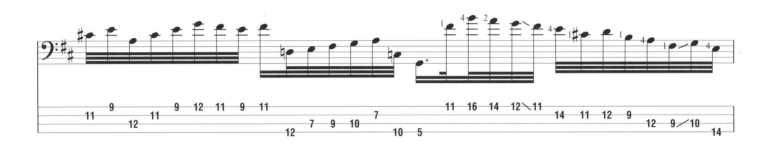

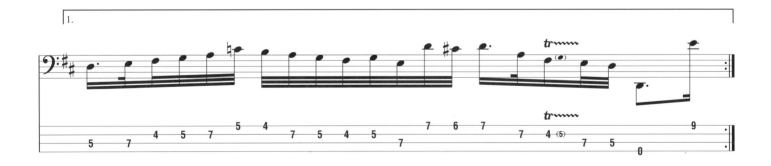

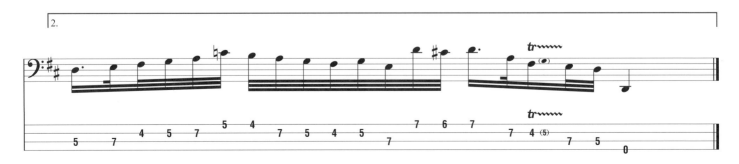

Courante

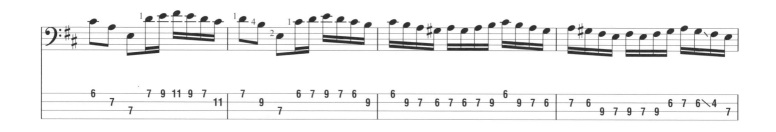

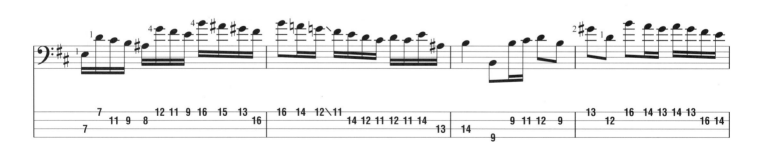

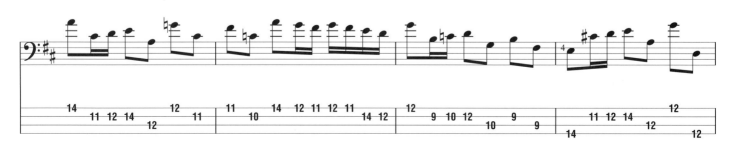

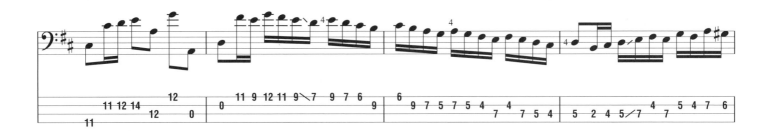

Sarabande

*w/ thumb & fingers

*Throughout, except where indicated.

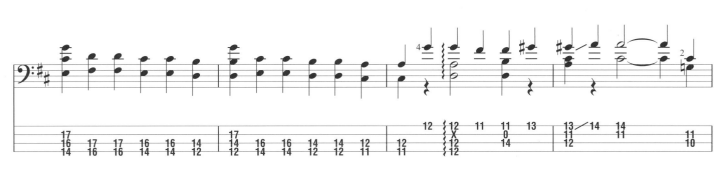

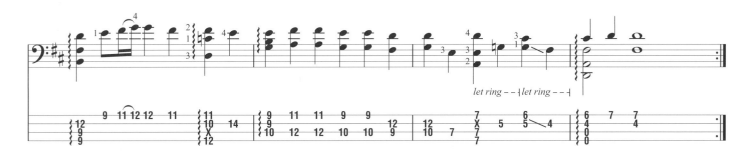

*w/ thumb & finger

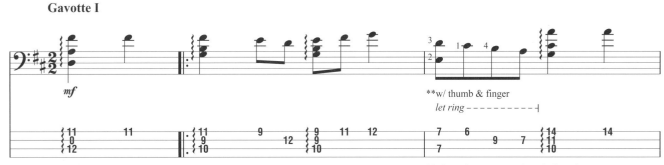

Gavotte I

**w/ thumb & finger

let ring - - - - - - - - -

**Throughout, except where indicated.

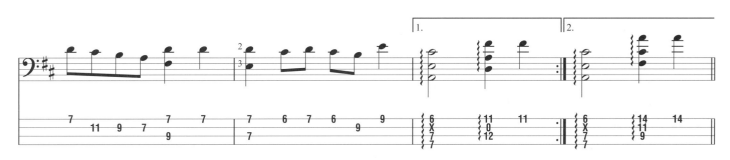

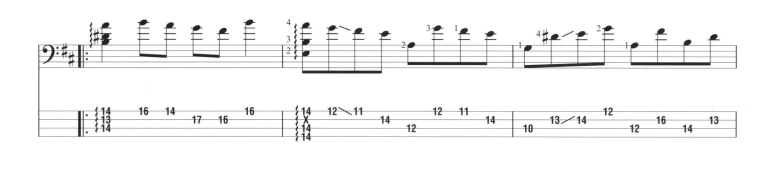

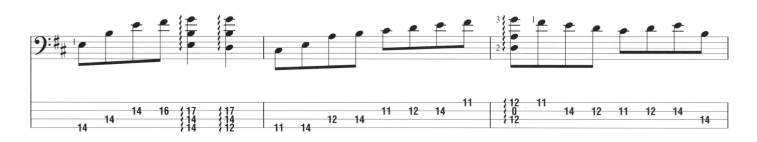

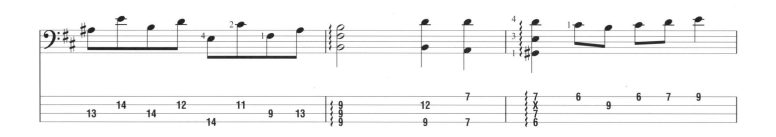

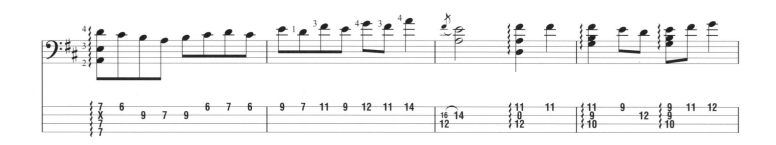

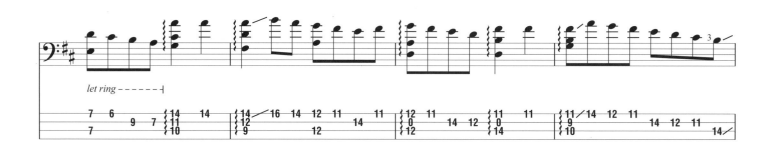

Gavotte II

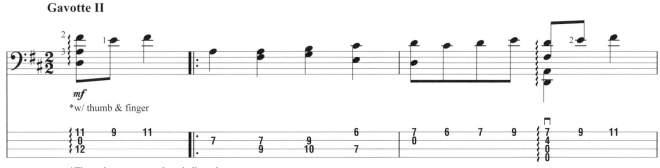

*w/ thumb & finger

*Throughout, except where indicated.

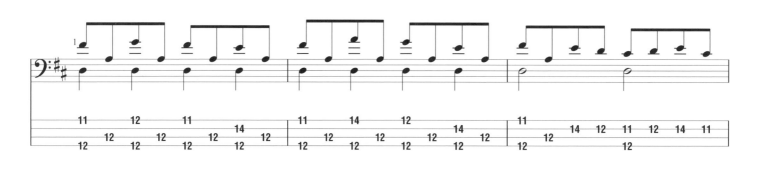

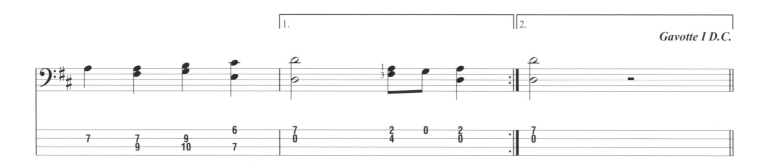

Gavotte I D.C.

Gigue

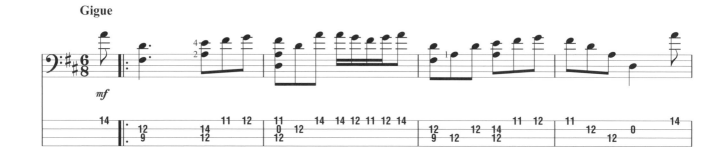

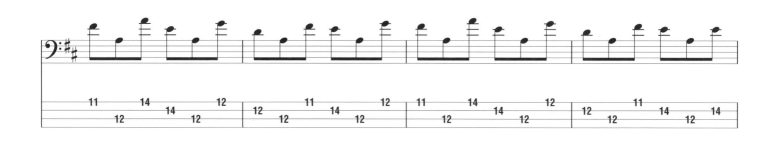

*w/ thumb & fingers

*Next 6 meas.

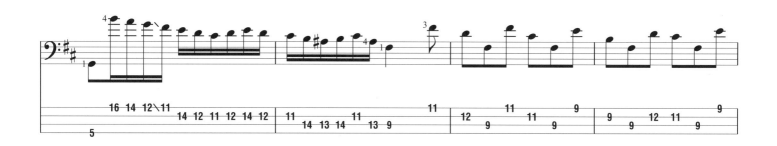

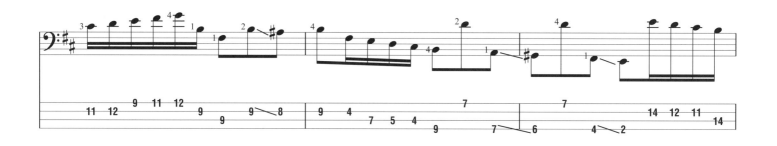

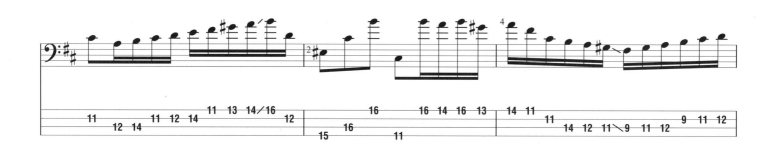

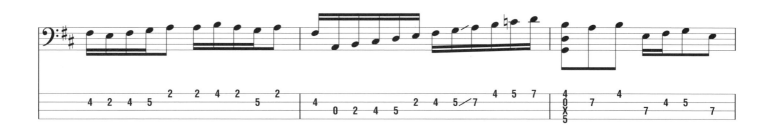

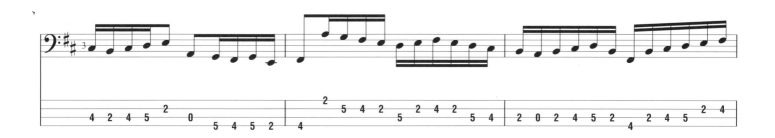

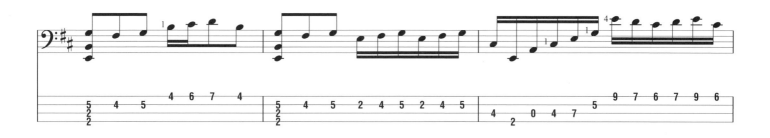

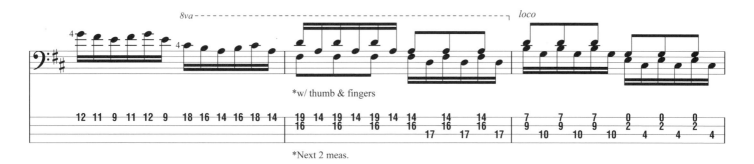

*w/ thumb & fingers

*Next 2 meas.

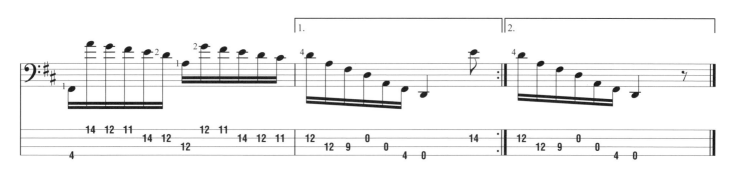

BASS NOTATION LEGEND

Bass music can be notated two different ways: on a *musical staff*, and in *tablature*.

THE MUSICAL STAFF shows pitches and rhythms and is divided by bar lines into measures. Pitches are named after the first seven letters of the alphabet.

TABLATURE graphically represents the bass fingerboard. Each horizontal line represents a string, and each number represents a fret.

3rd string, open   2nd string, 2nd fret   1st & 2nd strings open, played together

HAMMER-ON: Strike the first (lower) note with one finger, then sound the higher note (on the same string) with another finger by fretting it without picking.

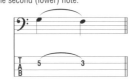

PULL-OFF: Place both fingers on the notes to be sounded. Strike the first note and without picking, pull the finger off to sound the second (lower) note.

LEGATO SLIDE: Strike the first note and then slide the same fret-hand finger up or down to the second note. The second note is not struck.

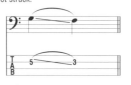

SHIFT SLIDE: Same as legato slide, except the second note is struck.

TRILL: Very rapidly alternate between the notes indicated by continuously hammering on and pulling off.

TREMOLO PICKING: The note is picked as rapidly and continuously as possible.

VIBRATO: The string is vibrated by rapidly bending and releasing the note with the fretting hand.

SHAKE: Using one finger, rapidly alternate between two notes on one string by sliding either a half-step above or below.

NATURAL HARMONIC: Strike the note while the fret hand lightly touches the string directly over the fret indicated.

MUFFLED STRINGS: A percussive sound is produced by laying the fret hand across the string(s) without depressing them and striking them with the pick hand.

BEND: Strike the note and bend up the interval shown.

BEND AND RELEASE: Strike the note and bend up as indicated, then release back to the original note. Only the first note is struck.

RIGHT-HAND TAP: Hammer ("tap") the fret indicated with the "pick-hand" index or middle finger and pull off to the note fretted by the fret hand.

LEFT-HAND TAP: Hammer ("tap") the fret indicated with the "fret-hand" index or middle finger.

SLAP: Strike ("slap") string with right-hand thumb.

POP: Snap ("pop") string with right-hand index or middle finger.

Additional Musical Definitions

 (accent)   • Accentuate note (play it louder).

 (accent)   • Accentuate note with great intensity.

 *(staccato)*   • Play the note short.

     • Downstroke

     • Upstroke

D.S. al Coda   • Go back to the sign (%), then play until the measure marked "*To Coda*," then skip to the section labelled "**Coda**."

D.C. al Fine   • Go back to the beginning of the song and play until the measure marked "*Fine*" (end).

Bass Fig.   • Label used to recall a recurring pattern.

Fill   • Label used to identify a brief melodic figure which is to be inserted into the arrangement.

tacet   • Instrument is silent (drops out).

     • Repeat measures between signs.

   • When a repeated section has different endings, play the first ending only the first time and the second ending only the second time.

NOTE: Tablature numbers in parentheses mean:
1. The note is being sustained over a system (note in standard notation is tied), or
2. The note is sustained, but a new articulation (such as a hammer-on, pull-off, slide or vibrato) begins.